40 Minute
BIBLE STUDIES

6-WEEK
STUDY PROGRAM

MONEY AND

———

POSSESSIONS:

———

THE QUEST FOR

———

CONTENTMENT

———

PRECEPT
MINISTRIES
INTERNATIONAL

KAY ARTHUR
& DAVID ARTHUR

MONEY AND POSSESSIONS: THE QUEST FOR CONTENTMENT
PUBLISHED BY WATERBROOK PRESS
2375 Telstar Drive, Suite 160
Colorado Springs, Colorado 80920
A division of Random House, Inc.

All Scripture quotations, unless otherwise indicated, are taken from the *New American Standard Bible®* (NASB). © Copyright The Lockman Foundation 1960, 1962, 1963, 1968, 1971, 1972, 1973, 1975, 1977, 1995. Used by permission. (www.Lockman.org).

Italics in Scripture quotations reflect the author's added emphasis.

ISBN 1-57856-906-0

Printed in the United States of America
2004—First Edition

10 9 8 7 6 5 4 3 2 1

HOW TO USE THIS STUDY

This small-group study is for people who are interested in learning for themselves more about what the Bible says on various subjects, but who have only limited time to meet together. It's ideal, for example, for a lunch group at work, an early morning men's group, a young mother's group meeting in a home, a Sunday-school class, or even family devotions. (It's also ideal for small groups that typically have longer meeting times—such as evening groups or Saturday morning groups—but want to devote only a portion of their time together to actual study, while reserving the rest for prayer, fellowship, or other activities.)

This book is designed so that all the group's participants will complete each lesson's study activities *at the same time.* Discussing your insights drawn from what God says about the subject reveals exciting, life-impacting truths.

Although it's a group study, you'll need a facilitator to lead the study and keep the discussion moving. (This person's function is *not* that of a lecturer or teacher. However, when this book is used in a Sunday-school class or similar setting, the teacher should feel free to lead more directly and to bring in other insights in addition to those provided in each week's lesson.)

If *you* are your group's facilitator, the leader, here are some helpful points for making your job easier:

- Go through the lesson and mark the text before you lead the group. This will give you increased familiarity with the material and will enable you to facilitate the group with greater ease. It may be easier for you to lead the group through the instructions for marking if you, as a leader, choose a specific color for each symbol you mark.

- As you lead the group, start at the beginning of the text and simply read it aloud in the order it appears in the lesson, including the "insight boxes," which appear throughout. Work through the lesson together, observing and discussing what you learn. As you read the Scripture verses, have the group say aloud the word they are marking in the text.

- The discussion questions are there simply to help you cover the material. As the class moves into the discussion, many times you will find that they will cover the questions on their own. Remember, the discussion questions are there to guide the group through the topic, not to squelch discussion.

- Remember how important it is for people to verbalize their answers and discoveries. This greatly strengthens their personal understanding of each week's lesson. Try to ensure that everyone has plenty of opportunity to contribute to each week's discussions.

- Keep the discussion moving. This may mean spending more time on some parts of the study than on others. If necessary, you should feel free to spread out a lesson over more than one session. However, remember that you don't want to slow the pace too much. It's much better to leave everyone "wanting more" than to have people dropping out because of declining interest.

- If the validity or accuracy of some of the answers seems questionable, you can gently and cheerfully remind the group to stay focused on the truth of the Scriptures. Your object is to learn what the Bible says, not to engage in human philosophy. Simply stick with the Scriptures and give God the opportunity to speak. His Word *is* truth (John 17:17)!

MONEY AND POSSESSIONS: THE QUEST FOR CONTENTMENT

The subject of money seems to be one of the most emotional issues of our times. For many of us, money rules like a despot over our attitudes, our time, our decisions, and our politics. An individual's personal economic status can cause his or her emotions to rise and fall like the stock market.

Money determines what we can buy, the things we can possess, the lifestyle we can attain and maintain. And we think we'll find contentment, if only we can accumulate enough.

Yet money is more than a measure of one's well being, the supposed security of one's future, or the means for bettering ourselves. The way a person handles money is a barometer of that individual's relationship with God. Money and possessions are a matter of the heart. They show where our true affections lie. This is why the New Testament devotes so much attention to money and possessions, for as Jesus said, "Where your treasure is, there your heart will be also" (Matthew 6:21).

In light of this truth, we need to know what God has to say about money, where it comes from, how we are to handle it, and what our accountability may be in respect to whatever we have. We hope you will find this study revolutionary and liberating as you gain new insights regarding your quest for contentment.

The psalmist declared that the earth and all it contains belongs to the Lord (Psalm 24:1). The book of James tells us that every good and perfect gift comes from our heavenly Father (1:17). Truly, all that we possess, even the air we breathe, is given to us by God.

As we read through the Gospels, we see Jesus reminding His followers frequently of their accountability to the Father. The writers of the Epistles also make it clear that how we choose to spend our time and resources can result either in God granting us rewards or declining to reward us when we meet Him face to face.

With all this in mind, we want to prepare for the day when we will give an account of what we have done with all we've been given, so that we are ready and unashamed.

OBSERVE

Let's begin by studying a parable told by Jesus in the final days of His earthly ministry.

A parable is a story which, although not usually factual, remains true to life and teaches a moral lesson or truth. To correctly interpret a parable you need to determine the occasion of the parable. Why was this parable told? What prompted it?

Luke 19:11 gives us the setting in which Jesus told this particular parable.

LUKE 19:11

11 While they were listening to these things, Jesus went on to tell a parable, because He was near Jerusalem, and they supposed that the kingdom of God was going to appear immediately.

Leader: *Read aloud Luke 19:11.*

• *Have the group mark every reference to* ***Jesus,*** *including pronouns, with a cross:* ✝ *Have the group say "Jesus" aloud each time they mark a reference to Him.*

DISCUSS

• Look at every place you marked *Jesus.* Where was Jesus when this incident took place?

• Why did He tell them a parable? (Look at what follows "because.")

LUKE 19:12-15

12 So He said "A nobleman went to a distant country to receive a kingdom for himself, and then return.

OBSERVE

Let's continue with the parable. Remember, Jesus is speaking in this passage.

Leader: *Read Luke 19:12-15 aloud. Have the group say aloud and…*

• *underline every reference to **the nobleman,** including pronouns.*

• *mark every word that indicates a sequence of **time**—then, when, until, after—with a clock, like this:* 🕐

DISCUSS

• Review the sequence of events in respect to the nobleman's comings and goings. What happened before he left and after his return?

• What did you learn from marking the references to the nobleman?

• In addition to the nobleman, who are the other two groups of people mentioned in this parable? Describe their relationship to the nobleman.

13 "And he called ten of his slaves, and gave them ten minas and said to them, 'Do business with this until I come back.'

14 "But his citizens hated him and sent a delegation after him, saying, 'We do not want this man to reign over us.'

15 "When he returned, after receiving the kingdom, he ordered that these slaves, to whom he had given the money, be called to him so that he might know what business they had done."

LUKE 19:12-25

12 So He said "A nobleman went to a distant country to receive a kingdom for himself, and then return.

13 "And he called ten of his slaves, and gave them ten minas and said to them, 'Do business with this until I come back.'

14 "But his citizens hated him and sent a delegation after him, saying, 'We do not want this man to reign over us.'

15 "When he returned, after receiving the kingdom, he ordered that these slaves, to whom he had given the money, be called to him so that he might know

OBSERVE

Leader: *Read Luke 19:12-25 and have the group do the following:*

- *Circle every reference to* **slave** *or* **slaves,** *including pronouns.*
- *Draw a box around every reference to* **minas** *and* **money,** *including pronouns.*

DISCUSS

- According to verse 13, how many slaves were there? And from what you read in verse 16, how many minas then were given to each slave?

- In respect to the nobleman's travels to a far country, when did he distribute the minas?

- What were the slaves to do with the minas?

• To whom did the minas belong?

• When were the slaves who were given the minas called to give an account to the nobleman?

• What right did the nobleman have to know what business the slaves have done while he was away?

• On what basis did the nobleman reward the slaves? Discuss his treatment of the three.

• Which of the three slaves received the greatest reward? Why do you think he received what he did? What was the percentage of the return on the nobleman's investment?

what business they had done.

16 "The first appeared, saying, 'Master, your mina has made ten minas more.'

17 "And he said to him, 'Well done, good slave, because you have been faithful in a very little thing, you are to be in authority over ten cities.'

18 "The second came, saying, 'Your mina, master, has made five minas.'

19 "And he said to him also, 'And you are to be over five cities.'

20 "Another came, saying, 'Master, here is your mina, which I kept put away in a handkerchief;

21 for I was afraid of you, because you are an exacting man; you take up what you did not lay down, and reap what you did not sow.'

22 "He said to him, 'By your own words I will judge you, you worthless slave. Did you know that I am an exacting man, taking up what I did not lay down, and reaping what I did not sow?

23 'Then why did you not put my money in the bank, and having come, I would have collected it with interest?'

24 "Then he said to the bystanders, 'Take the mina away from him and give it to the one who has the ten minas.'

• Why was the first given even more after the third slave gave his accounting?

• Do the nobleman's actions seem fair to you? Did they seem fair to the bystanders? What was their concern?

• Do you think people would respond the same way today? Why or why not?

• Do you think most people expect to receive the same treatment as others no matter what they do? Why?

• Do you think most people today have any concept of being accountable for how they handle their money or property? Why do you think this is?

OBSERVE

Now let's look at the conclusion of Jesus' parable.

Leader: Read Luke 19:26-27.
  • *Have the group mark every reference to **Jesus,** including pronouns, with a cross.*

DISCUSS

• How do Jesus' words in verse 26 relate to the response of the bystanders in the parable?

• Now, keeping in mind the setting and circumstances of this parable and what you've just read, whom do you think the nobleman in the parable represents? Explain your answer.

LUKE 19:26-27

25 "And they said to him, 'Master, he has ten minas already.'"

26 "I tell you that to everyone who has more, shall be given, but from the one who does not have, even what he does have shall be taken away.

27 "But these enemies of mine, who did not want me to reign over them, bring them here and slay them in my presence."

• Whom do you think the slaves represent?

• How does verse 26 relate to the slaves? According to Jesus, when rewards are given, who gets the most? Why?

• Do you see any correlation between the citizens of verse 14 and the enemies of verse 27? Explain your answer.

• Who are these people and what is their fate? According to this parable, when will this take place?

• What did you learn from this passage about our responsibility for what we have been given? How do you think we are supposed to use our money and material possessions?

OBSERVE

Let's contrast the slaves of Luke 19 with those who choose riches above God, people who want to control their own lives rather than be ruled by the Lord Jesus Christ.

Leader: *Read James 5:1-8 aloud. Have the group...*

- *draw a box around every reference to **the rich,** including pronouns:* ☐
- *mark every reference to **the times** with a clock:* 🕐
- *draw a cloud shape like this* ☁️ *around every reference to **the coming of the Lord.***

DISCUSS

- What did you learn from marking the references to the rich in verses 1-3? Don't miss a thing!

- Verses 4-6 mention at least three specific acts committed by the rich. Number and discuss each one.

JAMES 5:1-8

1 Come now, you rich, weep and howl for your miseries which are coming upon you.

2 Your riches have rotted and your garments have become moth-eaten.

3 Your gold and your silver have rusted; and their rust will be a witness against you and will consume your flesh like fire. It is in the last days that you have stored up your treasure!

4 Behold, the pay of the laborers who mowed your fields, and which has been withheld by you, cries out against you; and the outcry of those who did the harvesting

has reached the ears of the Lord of Sabaoth.

⁵ You have lived luxuriously on the earth and led a life of wanton pleasure; you have fattened your hearts in a day of slaughter.

⁶ You have condemned and put to death the righteous man; he does not resist you.

⁷ Therefore be patient, brethren, until the coming of the Lord. The farmer waits for the precious produce of the soil, being patient about it, until it gets the early and late rains.

⁸ You too be patient; strengthen your hearts, for the coming of the Lord is near.

• Have you seen similar behavior among those who pursue riches? If so, give an example.

OBSERVE

Leader: *Read aloud verses 7-8 of James 5 again. Have the group…*
- *circle every reference to* **the brethren,** *including pronouns.*
- *underline every reference to* **being patient.**

DISCUSS

• What did you learn from underlining the references to being patient? Who's supposed to be patient? What are they to do and why?

OBSERVE

Leader: *Have the group read Revelation 22:12 aloud.*

• *Mark every reference to **Jesus**, including pronouns, with a triangle:* △

DISCUSS

• What did you learn from marking the references to Jesus?

• On what basis will Jesus reward each individual?

• Discuss any parallels between this verse, Jesus' parable of the nobleman, and the passage regarding the rich man in James 5.

• According to what you have studied this week, what connection, if any, do you believe there will be between our money and our reward from Jesus?

• If Jesus were to return today, how prepared would you be to see Him and to give an account of what you have done with all He has given you?

REVELATION 22:12

[Jesus is speaking in this passage.]

12 Behold, I am coming quickly, and My reward is with Me, to render to every man according to what he has done.

WRAP IT UP

How easily we become preoccupied with money and the material things of this world! We tend to think that we have earned them by the sweat of our brow or the cleverness of our thinking, forgetting that everything we have comes from God. In truth, we are merely stewards, or custodians, of what He chooses to give us; and therefore, rich or poor, we will be held accountable to Him for what we do with it.

Second Corinthians 5:10 and Romans 14:10 tell us that Christians will one day stand at the judgment seat of Christ, where we will give an account of the works we have done. We will be called to explain what we have done with our lives, our gifts and abilities, and our monies and possessions. We have only a lifetime to serve God, and then we'll be rewarded for all eternity based on how we've handled our blessings here on earth. May God stamp eternity upon our eyes and remind us that when Jesus returns His reward will be with Him. What is one lifespan—seventy years or so—compared with all eternity?

Revelation 20:11-15 tells of God's judgment of those who remain dead in their trespasses and sins because they rejected life. They refused to believe in Jesus and receive Him as their Lord and their God, to have Him reign over them. Even in the lake of fire there will be degrees of punishment according to a person's deeds. God is just. Always. With all people.

In the light of these sobering truths, why don't you pause for a few minutes and quietly talk to the Lord—either in silence or as a group—about what you have learned.

Does your approach to money change when times are tough? Do God's expectations of you change when money is tight? Our study this week will help you answer those questions.

The books of 1 and 2 Chronicles were written after the children of Israel returned from exile to rebuild the temple that had been destroyed during the siege of the Babylonians in 586 B.C. The work of rebuilding was going very slowly. In fact, it had virtually stopped.

Times were tough for the people of God. The land had suffered a drought. They had sowed much but harvested little. Their clothing didn't keep them warm. Their purses seemed to have holes. They said they didn't have enough wood to build the temple of God—yet they had enough wood to build their own houses.

One of the purposes of Chronicles was to encourage the returned exiles by reminding them of when the first temple was built. The history related in Chronicles offered lessons intended to help them refocus their lives and get their priorities straight so they might receive a blessing from the Lord.

We, too, need to be aware of how God has moved among His people in the past, so that we might have a proper perspective of riches: their source and their purpose. Let's begin our study in 1 Chronicles 29. Then we will move to Haggai and hear what God said to His people when times were tough.

1 CHRONICLES 29:1-5

¹ Then King David said to the entire assembly, "My son Solomon, whom alone God has chosen, is still young and inexperienced and the work is great; for the temple is not for man, but for the LORD God.

² "Now with all my ability I have provided for the house of my God the gold for the things of gold, and the silver for the things of silver, and the bronze for the things of bronze, the iron for the things of iron, and wood for the things of wood, onyx stones and inlaid stones, stones of antimony and stones of various colors, and

OBSERVE

Leader: Read 1 Chronicles 29:1-5 aloud. As you read have the group...

- *underline every reference to **King David**, including the pronouns **I** and **my.***
- *draw a cloud like this around every reference to **the temple,** often called **the house of God.***

INSIGHT

Although David desired to build a permanent house for God, the Lord forbid him to do so because he had "shed much blood and...waged great wars" (1 Chronicles 22:8). However, God promised David that his son Solomon would build the temple. God then gave David all the details of the pattern of the structure, and David proceeded to gather the materials that would be needed for building the temple.

DISCUSS

• What did you learn from marking the references to David and the house of God?

• What did you learn from these verses about David's priorities?

all kinds of precious stones and alabaster in abundance.

3 "Moreover, in my delight in the house of my God, the treasure I have of gold and silver, I give to the house of my God, over and above all that I have already provided for the holy temple,

4 namely, 3,000 talents of gold, of the gold of Ophir, and 7,000 talents of refined silver, to overlay the walls of the buildings;

5 of gold for the things of gold and of silver for the things of silver, that is, for all the work done by the craftsmen. Who then is willing to consecrate himself this day to the LORD?"

1 CHRONICLES 29:5B-9

5 "Who then is willing to consecrate himself this day to the LORD?"

6 Then the rulers of the fathers' households, and the princes of the tribes of Israel, and the commanders of thousands and of hundreds, with the overseers over the king's work, offered willingly;

7 and for the service for the house of God they gave 5,000 talents and 10,000 darics of gold, and 10,000 talents of silver, and 18,000 talents of brass, and 100,000 talents of iron.

8 Whoever possessed precious stones gave them to the treasury of the house of the

OBSERVE

Leader: Read 1 Chronicles 29:5b-9. Have the group…

- *circle every reference to various **categories of people** such as rulers, commanders, etc. Include the pronouns, such as **who, whoever, they.***
- *draw a box around any reference to **offering** or **giving.***

DISCUSS

- According to verse 5, what did David call the people to do?

- How did they express their decision to obey David's request? What groups of people responded?

- What benefit would come from their actions, according to verse 7?

- What attitude was reflected in their actions?

• What caused the people and the king to rejoice?

• How does giving demonstrate a person's consecration to the Lord?

OBSERVE

Leader: Read 1 Chronicles 29:10-16 aloud. Have the group do the following:
- *Underline every reference to **David,** including pronouns.*
- *Circle every reference to **the people,** including the instances when David includes himself with the people.*
- *Draw a triangle △ over every occurrence of **God,** including the pronouns **You, Your, Yours.** (Do not mark any other references to God. These are enough to help you see what you need to see.)*

LORD, in care of Jehiel the Gershonite.

⁹ Then the people rejoiced because they had offered so willingly, for they made their offering to the LORD with a whole heart, and King David also rejoiced greatly.

1 CHRONICLES 29:10-16

¹⁰ So David blessed the LORD in the sight of all the assembly; and David said, "Blessed are You, O LORD God of Israel our father, forever and ever.

¹¹ "Yours, O LORD, is the greatness and the power and the glory and the victory and the majesty, indeed everything that is in the heavens and the earth; Yours is the

dominion, O LORD,
and You exalt Yourself
as head over all.

12 "Both riches and
honor come from You,
and You rule over all,
and in Your hand is
power and might; and
it lies in Your hand to
make great and to
strengthen everyone.

13 "Now therefore,
our God, we thank
You, and praise Your
glorious name.

14 "But who am I
and who are my
people that we should
be able to offer as gen-
erously as this? For all
things come from You,
and from Your hand
we have given You.

15 "For we are sojourn-
ers before You, and
tenants, as all our fathers

DISCUSS

• What did you learn about God from
marking the references to Him? Be sure
you don't miss a thing, as these are incredible truths.

• From what source did David and the children of Israel obtain what they gave to
God for the building of the temple?

• Summarize what you learned from these verses about money and possessions and about God's people.

OBSERVE

Let's continue our observations in 1 Chronicles. This next passage begins with David praying.

Leader: Read aloud 1 Chronicles 29:17-20,26-28. Have the group…
- *underline every reference to **David**, including the pronouns **I, my, he**.*
- *draw a heart like this ♡ over every occurrence of the word **heart**.*
- *circle every reference to **the people**.*

were; our days on the earth are like a shadow, and there is no hope.

16 "O LORD our God, all this abundance that we have provided to build You a house for Your holy name, it is from Your hand, and all is Yours."

1 CHRONICLES 29:17-20, 26-28

17 "Since I know, O my God, that You try the heart and delight in uprightness, I, in the integrity of my heart, have willingly offered all these things; so now with joy I have seen Your people, who are present here, make their offerings willingly to You.

18 "O LORD, the God of Abraham, Isaac and

Israel, our fathers,
preserve this forever
in the intentions of the
heart of Your people,
and direct their heart
to You;

¹⁹ and give to my son
Solomon a perfect
heart to keep Your
commandments, Your
testimonies and Your
statutes, and to do
them all, and to build
the temple, for which I
have made provision."

²⁰ Then David said
to all the assembly,
"Now bless the LORD
your God." And all
the assembly blessed
the LORD, the God of
their fathers, and
bowed low and did
homage to the LORD
and to the king.

DISCUSS

• What did you learn from marking the various references to the heart? What do you see in respect to the heart and giving?

• What did you learn about David from these verses?

• How was he described at the end of his life?

• Verse 17 says that God tries the heart. Do you think God tries our hearts in the area of money and our possessions? If so, what areas would He be examining in our lives today?

• Should a person be concerned about giving generously to God's work? Why?

• What does a person's level of giving reveal about his or her attitude toward money? What does it reflect about his or her relationship to God and His kingdom?

INSIGHT

The temple—provided for by King David and built by his son King Solomon—was destroyed by the Babylonians during the siege of Jerusalem in 586 B.C.

As prophesied by Jeremiah, the captivity of God's people under the Babylonians lasted seventy years. After Babylon was conquered by the Medes and the Persians, the king of Persia issued a decree for the Israelites to return to Jerusalem and rebuild their temple.

The book of Haggai was written after a remnant of the Jewish exiles returned from Babylon.

The work of rebuilding the temple began in 536 B.C. but stopped two years later in 534 B.C. Then God sent His prophet Haggai to speak to His people.

26 Now David the son of Jesse reigned over all Israel.

27 The period which he reigned over Israel was forty years; he reigned in Hebron seven years and in Jerusalem thirty-three years.

28 Then he died in a ripe old age, full of days, riches and honor; and his son Solomon reigned in his place.

HAGGAI 1:2-14; 2:8

2 "Thus says the LORD of hosts, 'This people says, "The time has not come, even the time for the house of the LORD to be rebuilt."'"

3 Then the word of the LORD came by Haggai the prophet, saying,

4 "Is it time for you yourselves to dwell in your paneled houses while this house lies desolate?"

5 Now therefore, thus says the LORD of hosts, "Consider your ways!

6 "You have sown much, but harvest little; you eat, but there is not enough to be satisfied; you drink, but there is

OBSERVE

Leader: Read aloud Haggai 1:2-14; 2:8. Have the group…

- *circle every reference to **the people**, including the pronouns **you, your**, and **he**.*

Leader: Now read through the passage again. This time have the group…

- *draw a triangle over every reference to **the Lord** or **the Lord of hosts**, including the pronouns **I** and **My**. (There is no need to mark any other references to God.)*
- *double underline every occurrence of the phrase **consider your ways**.*

DISCUSS

- In verse 2 what were the people saying regarding the house of the Lord?

- What does this passage tell you about the people's priorities?

- How did the Lord respond to them?

• If you compared how much money most people pour into their own homes with how much they invest in God's work for His kingdom in our days, where would you say our priorities are as children of God?

• When the Lord told the people to consider their ways in verses 5-7, what did He want them to recognize? The answer is in verse 6.

• What did you learn from marking references to the Lord in verses 9-11?

• What prompted God's actions?

not enough to become drunk; you put on clothing, but no one is warm enough; and he who earns, earns wages to put into a purse with holes."

7 Thus says the LORD of hosts, "Consider your ways!

8 "Go up to the mountains, bring wood and rebuild the temple, that I may be pleased with it and be glorified," says the LORD.

9 "You look for much, but behold, it comes to little; when you bring it home, I blow it away. Why?" declares the LORD of hosts, "Because of My house which lies desolate, while each of you runs to his own house.

10 "Therefore, because of you the sky has withheld its dew and the earth has withheld its produce.

11 "I called for a drought on the land, on the mountains, on the grain, on the new wine, on the oil, on what the ground produces, on men, on cattle, and on all the labor of your hands."

12 Then Zerubbabel the son of Shealtiel, and Joshua the son of Jehozadak, the high priest, with all the remnant of the people, obeyed the voice of the LORD their God and the words of Haggai the prophet, as the LORD their God had sent him. And the people showed reverence for the LORD.

• What insight do you find in this passage regarding a possible cause of tough times? (Note, we said "possible.")

• Would this passage give you any reason to stop and consider your ways when difficulties arise? Why?

• How did the people respond to the word of the Lord thru Haggai? What does this tell you about them?

• According to verses 13-14, what did God do following their response?

• What does Haggai 2:8 tell us? What does it reveal about who determines what we have?

• Whose money are you using when you purchase anything? How should that knowledge affect the way you spend your money?

• How does your spending compare with your giving? What percent of your income goes to the work of God?

• What truths has God spoken to your heart today?

13 Then Haggai, the messenger of the LORD, spoke by the commission of the LORD to the people saying, "'I am with you,' declares the LORD."

14 So the LORD stirred up the spirit of Zerubbabel the son of Shealtiel, governor of Judah, and the spirit of Joshua the son of Jehozadak, the high priest, and the spirit of all the remnant of the people; and they came and worked on the house of the LORD of hosts, their God.

2:8 "The silver is Mine and the gold is Mine," declares the LORD of hosts.

WRAP IT UP

Unlike the temple of Solomon in Haggai's time, the house of the Lord that is being built today is not a literal building; rather it is a living temple "being fitted together…growing into a holy temple in the Lord" with "Jesus Himself being the corner stone" (Ephesians 2:20-21). And we, beloved, have the responsibility and privilege of being used of God in building His church in evangelizing and discipling people from every tribe, tongue, and nation as we give to the work of the Lord.

What a sense of joy and contentment ought to flood our hearts as we realize that we have the privilege of being co-laborers together with God!

Given this amazing knowledge, one tends to wonder why more isn't being done. Why are churches, missions, and parachurch organizations always seeking more funding for their work?

Could it be that we, like the people in the days of Haggai, have failed to do what we are supposed to do? Are we more concerned about ourselves, about filling our houses with all the newest things, than about building the house of God? Have you asked yourself, "How much is enough for me personally? At what point do I stop accumulating and start giving more to God?"

Given our fluctuating economy, could it be we haven't prospered as we should because we have not made God's kingdom and His righteousness our top priorities?

On page 220 of his book *Racing Towards 2001: The Forces Shaping America's Religious Future,* Russell Chandler writes, "If church members were to boost their giving an average of 10 percent of their income (the tithe), the additional funds could eliminate the worst of world poverty…plus another $17 billion for domestic need—all while maintaining church activities at all current levels." All that could be accomplished by giving just 10 percent of our income!

According to what we have seen in the Word of God just in these first two weeks of study, all we have comes from God. We simply give to God out of the abundance of all He has given to us.

Does this cause you to wonder what would happen in our lives if God's work became our first priority? Why don't you determine to find out?

When a person genuinely turns to the Lord, should that change his or her approach to money, personal possessions, and the quest for contentment? In what ways does a real relationship with God impact our values? Is there any effect on our attitude and handling of our money, investments, and possessions—or are those areas of no real concern to God?

OBSERVE

Let's begin by looking at a message from John the Baptist as he was preaching in the area around the Jordan River.

Leader: Read Luke 3:9-14 aloud. Have the group...
- *underline every occurrence of **he** and **him,** both of which are references to **John.***
- *circle every reference to **the crowds, individuals,** and various **groups of people** to whom John is speaking.*

DISCUSS

- What was John warning his listeners about in verse 9?

LUKE 3:9-14

9 "Indeed the axe is already laid at the root of the trees; so every tree that does not bear good fruit is cut down and thrown into the fire."

10 And the crowds were questioning him, saying, "Then what shall we do?"

11 And he would answer and say to them, "The man who has two tunics is to share with him who has none; and he who has food is to do likewise."

12 And some tax collectors also came to be baptized, and they said to him, "Teacher, what shall we do?"

13 And he said to them, "Collect no more than what you have been ordered to."

14 Some soldiers were questioning him, saying, "And what about us, what shall we do?" And he said to them, "Do not take money from anyone by force, or accuse anyone falsely, and be content with your wages."

• What did you learn from circling the references to the people? What different groups were present?

• What question did each of the groups ask in response to John's warning?

• What did John instruct each group to do?

• What did John's answers in verses 11, 13, and 14 have in common with each other? In each situation, what theme does John touch on?

OBSERVE

Luke 19 describes as Jesus' encounter with Zaccheus as He was passing through Jericho on His way to Jerusalem. Zaccheus was a chief tax collector, a rich man. Luke 19:8-10 details what happened after Jesus told Zaccheus that He was going to his house.

Leader: *Read Luke 19:8-10 aloud. Have the group...*

- *circle every reference to* **Zaccheus**, *including the pronouns* **he** *and* **I.**
- *draw a triangle over every reference to* **Jesus**, *including synonyms such as* **Lord** *and* **Son of Man.**

INSIGHT

The Jews looked upon tax gatherers as traitors because they collected money on behalf of the Romans who ruled over their nation. Because of their lifestyle and their greed, tax collectors often overtaxed their own people and pocketed the extra money. Consequently, such men were greatly despised by their fellow Jews.

DISCUSS

- According to verse 8, what impact did Jesus' presence and attention have on Zaccheus? What was Zaccheus's response to Jesus? In what area was Zaccheus convicted?

LUKE 19:8-10

8 Zaccheus stopped and said to the Lord, "Behold, Lord, half of my possessions I will give to the poor, and if I have defrauded anyone of anything, I will give back four times as much."

9 And Jesus said to him, "Today salvation has come to this house, because he, too, is a son of Abraham.

10 "For the Son of Man has come to seek and to save that which was lost."

• What parallel do you see, if any, between what John the Baptist told the people to do and how Zaccheus responded to Christ? Does this incident tell you anything about how a man's relationship with God affects his attitude toward what he possesses or the value he places on his money? Explain your answer.

• According to verse 9, what happened to Zaccheus that day?

MARK 10:17-23

17 As He was setting out on a journey, a man ran up to Him and knelt before Him, and asked Him, "Good Teacher, what shall I do to inherit eternal life?"

18 And Jesus said to him, "Why do you call Me good? No one is good except God alone.

OBSERVE

Three of the Gospels relate an incident when Jesus was approached by a man who has come to be known to Bible students as the "rich young ruler."

Leader: Read Mark 10:17-23 aloud. Have the group...
- *draw a triangle over every reference to **Jesus,** including pronouns and synonyms such as **Teacher.** Begin with **He** in verse 17.*
- *circle every reference to **the man,** including pronouns.*

DISCUSS

• Briefly discuss the events recorded in these verses. Why did the man come to Jesus?

• What did you learn about the character of this man and his lifestyle from marking references to him in the text?

• According to verse 21, how did Jesus feel about him?

• According to Jesus, what was the one thing this man lacked?

• What did Jesus tell him to do and how did he respond?

• What does this tell you about the man's attitude toward his possessions? What held first place in his heart?

• What opportunity did he miss and why?

• Where did this man think he would find contentment?

19 "You know the commandments, 'Do not murder, Do not commit adultery, Do not steal, Do not bear false witness, Do not defraud, Honor your father and mother.'"

20 And he said to Him, "Teacher, I have kept all these things from my youth up."

21 Looking at him, Jesus felt a love for him and said to him, "One thing you lack: go and sell all you possess and give to the poor, and you will have treasure in heaven; and come, follow Me."

22 But at these words he was saddened, and he went away grieving, for he was one who owned much property.

23 And Jesus, looking around, said to His disciples, "How hard it will be for those who are wealthy to enter the kingdom of God!"

• According to Jesus' words in verse 23, what is the danger of wealth? Why?

• How does this incident compare with the passages of Scripture we studied regarding John the Baptist and Jesus' encounter with Zaccheus? What's the common factor or recurring issue in each passage?

• What have you learned about the role of money and possessions in respect to an individual's relationship with God and His Son, Jesus Christ?

LUKE 12:16-21

16 And He told them a parable, saying, "The land of a rich man was very productive.

17 "And he began reasoning to himself, saying, 'What shall I do, since I have no place to store my crops?'

OBSERVE

Let's look at a passage in Luke that records another of Jesus' parables, this one on the topic of saving up material wealth. Jesus told this parable after a person in the crowd asked Jesus to instruct his brother to divide the family inheritance with him.

Leader: *Read Luke 12:16-21. Have the group...*

- *underline every reference to **the rich man,** including pronouns.*
- *draw a triangle over every reference to **God.***

DISCUSS

- What did you learn from marking the references to the rich man?

- What had he decided to do with his possessions? Why? What was his thinking?

- How did God respond to him? What did He tell the rich man?

- What would happen to the rich man's possessions when he died? Could he take them with him?

- Will the same be true of your possessions when you die?

18 "Then he said, 'This is what I will do: I will tear down my barns and build larger ones, and there I will store all my grain and my goods.

19 'And I will say to my soul, "Soul, you have many goods laid up for many years to come; take your ease, eat, drink and be merry."'

20 "But God said to him, 'You fool! This very night your soul is required of you; and now who will own what you have prepared?'

21 "So is the man who stores up treasure for himself, and is not rich toward God."

LUKE 12:15

15 Then He said to them, "Beware, and be on your guard against every form of greed; for not even when one has an abundance does his life consist of his possessions."

OBSERVE

Let's back up one verse to be sure we get the point.

Leader: Read Luke 12:15 aloud.

DISCUSS

• What warning did Jesus give to the crowd and the man who approached Him?

LUKE 12:33-34

33 "Sell your possessions and give to charity; make yourselves money belts which do not wear out, an unfailing treasure in heaven, where no thief comes near nor moth destroys.

34 For where your treasure is, there your heart will be also."

OBSERVE

If life isn't about attaining wealth, then what goal should we have? Let's look at what Jesus told His disciples later in this same chapter.

Leader: Have the group read Luke 12:33-34 aloud.

DISCUSS

• What are Jesus' instructions in verse 33?

• What are "money belts which do not wear out"? Look carefully at verse 33.

• If the disciples obeyed Jesus' instructions, where would their treasure be? What was His promise regarding that treasure?

• What does that tell you about the permanency of their treasure?

• How does this compare with treasure of the rich man in the parable?

• What does a person's "investment strategy" reveal about his or her heart?

• According to all you've learned, do you think leaving your "estate"—whether large or small—to your children, to worldly charities, or to whatever the government might decide to do with it, would be pleasing to God? Why or why not?

• Do your thoughts and concerns tend to center on where you invest your time, your talents, your treasure? What does that reveal about your own priorities?

ACTS 2:37-38,41-45

37 Now when they heard this, they were pierced to the heart, and said to Peter and the rest of the apostles, "Brethren, what shall we do?"

38 Peter said to them, "Repent, and each of you be baptized in the name of Jesus Christ for the forgiveness of your sins; and you will receive the gift of the Holy Spirit."

41 So then, those who had received his word were baptized; and that day there were added about three thousand souls.

42 They were continually devoting themselves to the apostles'

OBSERVE

The following passage begins just after Peter delivers the gospel—the message of the death, burial, and resurrection of Jesus Christ—to those who came to Jerusalem to celebrate the Feast of Pentecost.

Leader: *Read Acts 2:37-38,41-45. Have the group do the following:*

- *Circle every reference to **the people**, including the pronouns **they, we, you, those, everyone.***
- *Put a mark like this* *around the word **repent**.*
- *Put a heart over the word **heart:*** ♡

INSIGHT

The word *repent* in the Greek comes from two words that mean "to have a change of mind, of thinking." A true change of mind affects a person's beliefs and/or behavior.

DISCUSS

• What did you learn from marking the references to the people?

• How did their belief in Jesus affect their attitude toward their possessions?

• Note the tense of the verb in verse 45; in the Greek "began selling and sharing" is a present active participle, indicating a continuous or repeated action. So does this verse indicate that they sold everything immediately or as the need arose?

• How do the actions of these believers relate to what you have seen this week in respect to the connection between a person's salvation and his or her handling of money and possessions?

teaching and to fellowship, to the breaking of bread and to prayer.

43 Everyone kept feeling a sense of awe; and many wonders and signs were taking place through the apostles.

44 And all those who had believed were together and had all things in common;

45 and they began selling their property and possessions and were sharing them with all, as anyone might have need.

Acts 4:32-35

32 And the congregation of those who believed were of one heart and soul; and not one of them claimed that anything belonging to him was his own, but all things were common property to them.

33 And with great power the apostles were giving testimony to the resurrection of the Lord Jesus, and abundant grace was upon them all.

34 For there was not a needy person among them, for all who were owners of land or houses would sell them and bring the proceeds of the sales

OBSERVE

Leader: Read Acts 4:32-35 aloud. Have the group...

• *circle every reference to **the believers,** including all pronouns, whether singular or plural.*

• *draw a heart over the word **heart.***

DISCUSS

• What did you learn from marking the references to the believers? How would you characterize their attitude?

• Why was there "not a needy person among" the believers?

• What does this reveal about their hearts? On what were they focused?

OBSERVE

Leader: Read Acts 5:1-6. Have the group…
• *underline every reference to **Ananias**.*
• *put a dollar sign like this $ over any reference to **sold** or **price**.*

DISCUSS

• Review what happens in this passage. What did you learn from marking the references to Ananias?

• Did Ananias die because he held back some of the money or for another reason? The correct answer to this question is important. Look at the entire text for the answer.

ACTS 5:1-6

35 and lay them at the apostles' feet, and they would be distributed to each as any had need.

1 But a man named Ananias, with his wife Sapphira, sold a piece of property,

2 and kept back some of the price for himself, with his wife's full knowledge, and bringing a portion of it, he laid it at the apostles' feet.

3 But Peter said, "Ananias, why has Satan filled your heart to lie to the Holy Spirit and to keep back some of the price of the land?

4 "While it remained unsold, did it not remain your own? And after it was sold, was it not under your control? Why is it that you have conceived this deed in your heart? You have not lied to men but to God."

5 And as he heard these words, Ananias fell down and breathed his last; and great fear came over all who heard of it.

6 The young men got up and covered him up, and after carrying him out, they buried him.

• In the two previous passages in Acts we saw that those who believed at the Feast of Pentecost were so greatly affected that they sold what they had and gave it to those in need. Is this to be the standard for all believers? When we become Christians, are we to literally sell everything we have and give it to the church to distribute? Are we to have no investments or possessions of our own? Or do these events reflect an attitude, a heart focused on God and the people of God? Look at verse 4 and discuss how this answers the question.

• After you repented and believed in the Lord Jesus Christ, was there any change in the way you viewed possessions, money, the needs of others, and the work of God? Share your experience with the group.

• If there is time, summarize what you learned these past three weeks regarding what should be the believer's attitude toward money and possessions.

WRAP IT UP

It's quite evident from the Word of God that our relationship with Jesus Christ affects how we view every aspect of life, including our money and possessions. It's also patently clear in the account of the "rich young ruler," as he is described in Matthew and Luke, that if you are not willing to surrender all to Jesus Christ—including your material wealth—you cannot enter the kingdom of heaven. When Jesus told the young ruler that no one was good but God, He was pointing out that, as God, He deserved his full worship and devotion—yet the ruler was holding back.

The ruler was a fine young man who claimed to have kept all the commandments, but in fact he had broken the first commandment: He had put wealth above God. Jesus wanted him to recognize his idolatry and walk away from it, but he wouldn't. He could not bear to leave his riches and follow Jesus. He loved his wealth more than he loved God and His kingdom, so this young man missed out on eternal life.

Have you ever wondered what would have happened if only he had chosen to surrender to God what already belonged to Him? The ruler could have had riches untold as an heir of God and a joint heir with Jesus. Instead he held on to what he could see in this temporal life. If he lived another forty years, which was likely, all he held on to in his quest for contentment was destroyed when Titus besieged and destroyed Jerusalem in A.D. 70.

Don't miss this point: Jesus loved this young man yet He let him walk away. As he chose temporal wealth over eternal life, Jesus made an observation recorded in His eternal Word for all generations to read. It's a timely warning: It is hard for the wealthy to enter the kingdom. Riches can become our god, and God will not tolerate any other gods before Him.

It's clear from what we've studied that when God touches your heart in salvation, He touches your wallet as well. The joy of loving God and His people increases your sensitivity to people's needs. Your heart burns with the importance of getting the message of the gospel out to the whole world and teaching them the whole counsel of God. That's what the early church was all about, and they demonstrated their devotion through their giving!

Salvation affects even the way we view our possessions. Does this mean we are obligated to immediately sell everything we own and give it away? No, this is not supported in the rest of Scripture. The account of Ananias and Sapphira, which we studied in part, confirms that what we have and what we sell is in our control. And that won't be a problem as long as we are under God's control. Our responsibility is to have a sensitive, listening heart, quick to do whatever God says. We're to make money belts that won't wear out!

How does a person do that? We explore that and much more in the following three weeks.

What do you treasure most in life? When you look at where you spend the bulk of your time, energies, and money, you can get a true measure of your heart. Our goal this week will be to see what Jesus said about a person's treasures and, in doing so, to drop a plumb line so each of us can determine how we individually measure up to His precepts for life. Since the way we live will impact our eternal reward, we are wise to prepare now by assessing our priorities in light of His Word. Let's begin with Jesus' message to His disciples delivered on a mountain overlooking the Sea of Galilee. Jesus had just finished talking to them about giving, praying, and fasting. Next He turned to the issue of treasures.

OBSERVE

Leader: Read Matthew 6:19-24 and have the group...

- *circle every reference to* **those listening** *to the message of Jesus, including words such as* **yourselves, your, you, no one,** *and* **he.**
- *draw a box around every reference to* **treasures** *or* **wealth.**
- *draw a heart over the words* **heart** *and* **love.**

MATTHEW 6:19-24

19 "Do not store up for yourselves treasures on earth, where moth and rust destroy, and where thieves break in and steal.

20 "But store up for yourselves treasures in heaven, where neither moth nor rust destroys, and where thieves do not break in or steal;

21 for where your treasure is, there your heart will be also.

22 "The eye is the lamp of the body; so then if your eye is clear, your whole body will be full of light.

23 "But if your eye is bad, your whole body will be full of darkness. If then the light that is in you is darkness, how great is the darkness!

24 "No one can serve two masters; for either he will hate the one and love the other, or he will be devoted to one and despise the other. You cannot serve God and wealth."

DISCUSS

• What did you learn from marking the references to those who were listening to Jesus?

• What's the connection between one's heart and one's treasures? What does this have to do with God?

• What does a person's attitude toward money and possessions reveal about his or her relationship with God and understanding of eternal things?

• What are some ways people store up treasures—on earth or in heaven—today?

OBSERVE

In the passage we just examined, Jesus mentioned the eyes as well as the heart. To understand the significance of this, let's look at another passage of Scripture.

Leader: Read 1 John 2:15-16. Have the group...
- *draw a heart over every reference to love.*
- *circle each occurrence of the word world.*

DISCUSS

- What did you learn from marking the references to the world?

- What three things did the apostle John list as being from the world? Number them in the text and discuss them.

- How might these three things be manifested in a person's life? Give examples of each.

1 JOHN 2:15-16

15 Do not love the world nor the things in the world. If anyone loves the world, the love of the Father is not in him.

16 For all that is in the world, the lust of the flesh and the lust of the eyes and the boastful pride of life, is not from the Father, but is from the world.

• According to these verses, what prevents a person from loving God?

OBSERVE

Leader: *Return to pages 47-48 and read Matthew 6:19-24 aloud once more.*

DISCUSS

• From what we have seen in 1 John 2, why do you think Jesus spoke to His listeners about both the heart and the eye in the context of treasures and serving two masters? What point did Jesus want to make? What causes us to desire earthly treasures?

• So how does a person's focus impact his or her spiritual life—and eternal reward?

INSIGHT

In the original Greek, the verb translated as *serve* in Matthew 6:24 is in the present tense, indicating continual or habitual action.

• What two masters did Jesus mention?

• What's the bottom line Jesus wanted His followers to understand regarding treasures and spiritual matters?

• What evidence have you observed—in your own life or others'—that confirms His statement in verse 24?

• How would the choices we make in life reflect a sincere belief that His statement is true? Discuss practical ways in which this would guide our decisions.

OBSERVE

Let's continue with Jesus' message in Matthew.

Leader: Read Matthew 6:25-34. Have the group do the following:
- *Circle every reference to **the people**, including every **you, your,** and **we.***
- *Mark every reference to **God** with a triangle: △*

MATTHEW 6:25-34

25 "For this reason I say to you, do not be worried about your life, as to what you will eat or what you will drink; nor for your body, as to what you will put on. Is not life more than food, and the body more than clothing?

26 "Look at the birds of the air, that they do not sow, nor reap nor gather into barns, and yet your heavenly Father feeds them. Are you not worth much more than they?

27 "And who of you by being worried can add a single hour to his life?

28 "And why are you worried about clothing? Observe how the lilies of the field grow; they do not toil nor do they spin,

29 yet I say to you that not even Solomon in all his glory clothed himself like one of these.

30 "But if God so clothes the grass of the field, which is alive today and tomorrow is

• *Underline every phrase about **being worried or anxious** and **every instruction not to worry.***

DISCUSS

• What did you learn from marking the references to those listening to Jesus? What did He want them to know and to do? Why?

• Look at every reference about being anxious or worried. What did you learn?

• What did Jesus want His followers to understand about God the Father from these verses? Do you think what Jesus was saying is true? Why?

• How does this compare with what Jesus taught about not laying up treasures on earth?

thrown into the furnace, will He not much more clothe you? You of little faith!

31 "Do not worry then, saying, 'What will we eat?' or 'What will we drink?' or 'What will we wear for clothing?'

• What command and promise do we find in verse 33?

32 "For the Gentiles eagerly seek all these things; for your heavenly Father knows that you need all these things.

33 "But seek first His kingdom and His righteousness, and all these things will be added to you.

• What do you think it means to "seek first His kingdom and His righteousness"? How would this attitude be reflected in our daily lives? Give several practical examples.

34 "So do not worry about tomorrow; for tomorrow will care for itself. Each day has enough trouble of its own."

1 TIMOTHY 6:8-11,17-19

8 If we have food and covering, with these we shall be content.

9 But those who want to get rich fall into temptation and a snare and many foolish and harmful desires which plunge men into ruin and destruction.

10 For the love of money is a root of all sorts of evil, and some by longing for it have wandered away from the faith and pierced themselves with many griefs.

11 But flee from these things, you man of God, and pursue righteousness, godliness, faith, love, perseverance and gentleness.

OBSERVE

Thus far we've learned that God wants us to trust Him to care for our needs. But what if you desire to be rich or you already are rich? What does God say? That is what we'll look at next.

Leader: Read 1 Timothy 6:8-11 and verses 17-19. Have the group do the following:
- *Circle the references to **we** and to **the man of God**.*
- *Underline every reference to **those who want to get rich** or **who are rich**, including pronouns.*
- *Draw a heart over the word **love**.*
- *Draw a box around every reference to **money, riches, and treasure**.*

DISCUSS

• What did you observe from marking *we*? What is God's instruction, and how does it compare with what you observed in Matthew 6? With what are we to be content?

• What did you learn about those who want to be rich?

• What is God's word to us in verse 11? What are we to flee? What are we to pursue? How would this "play out" practically today?

• What did you learn about riches in verse 17?

• What are God's instructions for those who are rich?

• In light of all you have learned since beginning this study, what do you think God means when He mentions storing up "the treasure for the good foundation for the future"? Explain your answer.

• Carefully read the text once more. Is money evil? Is it a sin to have money? What distinction, if any, does God make between those who are rich and those who pursue wealth?

• According to all you have learned, where will you or anyone else find true contentment?

17 Instruct those who are rich in this present world not to be conceited or to fix their hope on the uncertainty of riches, but on God, who richly supplies us with all things to enjoy.

18 Instruct them to do good, to be rich in good works, to be generous and ready to share,

19 storing up for themselves the treasure of a good foundation for the future, so that they may take hold of that which is life indeed.

MARK 4:18-20

18 "And others are the ones on whom seed was sown among the thorns; these are the ones who have heard the word,

19 but the worries of the world, and the deceitfulness of riches, and the desires for other things enter in and choke the word, and it becomes unfruitful.

20 And those are the ones on whom seed was sown on the good soil; and they hear the word and accept it and bear fruit, thirty, sixty, and a hundredfold."

OBSERVE

We're going to look at a portion of another of Jesus' parables, this one focusing on the sowing of seed. In the parable of the sower, Jesus gave four different scenarios to describe what happens when the Word of God, the seed, is sown in the heart of man. Jesus described four different soils, each revealing the varied responses of people to the Word of God. In each incident, the seed is the constant; the variance is the soil. Only one soil, the fourth, represents that of a genuine believer. In this particular part of the parable, we will look at the third and fourth soils as explained by Jesus.

Leader: *Read Mark 4:18-20. Have the group...*

- *mark every reference to **the Word** (speaking of the Word of God) with a symbol like a book:*
- *draw a box around any reference to **riches** or **possessions**.*

DISCUSS

• According to verse 19, what are the three thorns that choke the Word of God in a person's life? Number those three things in the text and describe each one.

• What happens to the Word of God when it is sown among these thorns?

• Discuss an instance when you have seen this take place in someone's life.

• How is the fourth soil described in verse 20?

• What causes the difference between the yields described in verse 19 and in verse 20?

• How might this relate to Jesus' words in Revelation 22:12: "Behold, I am coming quickly, and My reward is with Me, to render to every man according to what he has done"? Will some receive greater rewards than others? On what basis?

• Which verse best describes the soil of your heart and the harvest of your life?

DEUTERONOMY 8:11-14

11 "Beware that you do not forget the LORD your God by not keeping His commandments and His ordinances and His statutes which I am commanding you today;

12 otherwise, when you have eaten and are satisfied, and have built good houses and lived in them,

13 and when your herds and your flocks multiply, and your silver and gold multiply, and all that you have multiplies,

14 then your heart will become proud and you will forget the LORD your God who

OBSERVE

Recognizing the dangers that accompany prosperity, God gave a warning to His people as they prepared, in fulfillment of His promise to Abraham, Isaac, and Jacob, to take possession of Canaan. Let's look at that warning, given through Moses, God's servant and Israel's leader.

Leader: Read Deuteronomy 8:11-14. Have the group...
- *circle every pronoun that refers to **the Israelites.***
- *draw a triangle over every reference to **God,** including pronouns.*

DISCUSS

• What was God's warning to the people through Moses?

• What might cause them to forget God? What did He say they must be careful to do?

• What personal dangers would they face?

• What lessons do you find in these verses for us today?

OBSERVE

Leader: Read Luke 12:15. Have the group...

• *draw a box around Jesus' instructions to His followers.*

DISCUSS

• What was Jesus' instruction?

• How do you believe most people define happiness, contentment, and fulfillment?

• How does their definition correspond to or conflict with Jesus' statement in Luke 12:15?

brought you out from the land of Egypt, out of the house of slavery."

LUKE 12:15

15 Then He said to them, "Beware, and be on your guard against every form of greed; for not even when one has an abundance does his life consist of his possessions."

COLOSSIANS 3:5-6

5 Therefore consider the members of your earthly body as dead to immorality, impurity, passion, evil desire, and greed, which amounts to idolatry.

6 For it is because of these things that the wrath of God will come upon the sons of disobedience.

OBSERVE

Leader: Read Colossians 3:5-6 and have the group…

- *draw a tombstone over the word **dead**, like this:* ⌂
- *draw a box around the word **greed**.*

DISCUSS

• What did you learn from marking *greed*?

• How does God feel about idols? Does He condone them?

• How is a Christian to respond to the temptation of greed?

ECCLESIASTES 5:10

10 He who loves money will not be satisfied with money, nor he who loves abundance with its income. This too is vanity.

OBSERVE

Leader: Read Ecclesiastes 5:10 aloud. Have the group…

- *mark every occurrence of **loves** with a heart.*
- *draw a box around every reference to **money** and **abundance**.*

DISCUSS

• What did you learn from this verse about loving money and abundance?

• Does the quest for money bring contentment?

• From what you've observed, has this proven to be true? How?

OBSERVE

Leader: *Read Ecclesiastes 5:13-16 aloud. Have the group...*

> • *draw a box around every reference to* **riches.**
> • *underline every occurrence of the phrase* **grievous evil.**

DISCUSS

• What did you learn from marking *grievous evil*? Discuss them one by one.

• What is the first grievous evil?

ECCLESIASTES 5:13-16

13 There is a grievous evil which I have seen under the sun: riches being hoarded by their owner to his hurt.

14 When those riches were lost through a bad investment and he had fathered a son, then there was nothing to support him.

15 As he had come naked from his mother's womb, so will he

return as he came. He will take nothing from the fruit of his labor that he can carry in his hand.

16 This also is a grievous evil—exactly as a man is born, thus will he die. So what is the advantage to him who toils for the wind?

• You've heard the expression "you can't take it with you." What in this passage supports that?

• What is the second grievous evil? Explain verse 16 in your own words.

• In the light of this and all that you have learned this week, what is the eternal value of earthly riches and material wealth?

• What kind of treasures can we store up now for eternity?

WRAP IT UP

When the devil tempted Jesus and challenged Him, after forty days of fasting, to make bread out of stones and fulfill His own basic needs, Jesus replied, "It is written, 'Man shall not live on bread alone, but on every word that proceeds out of the mouth of God' " (Matthew 4:4). "Every word" means the whole Bible!

When the devil offered Jesus all the kingdoms of this world and its riches, once again He countered with the sword of the Spirit, quoting the Word of God.

Beloved, the only way to keep the treasures of this world in proper perspective is through knowing and obeying the Word of God. The Word keeps eternity before your eyes.

So how are you doing? What are you living on? What priority does God's Word have in your life? And what will you tell God when you see Him face to face and give an account of the way you lived? Is your life directed by every word that God spoke and recorded in His Book so that, through His power, you might have everything you need pertaining to life and godliness (2 Peter 1:3)?

Pursuing riches, catering to our fleshly desires, laying up treasures on earth—all of these prevent us from really getting to know and study God's Book, don't they? You can't serve God while pursuing wealth; both are a full-time job!

In Matthew 6, after urging His followers to lay up treasures in heaven rather than on earth, Jesus declared that not only is God responsible to take care of our basic needs, He is fully capable of doing so. God will meet our every need if only we will make Him our priority, if we seek His kingdom and His righteousness before and above anything else.

Please don't misunderstand; there's absolutely nothing wrong with having money. The only problem is loving it or not being a good and responsible steward of it! God makes rich and He makes poor. He can take riches away in a moment if He desires. He is God. The earth is His and so is everything in it, and He can bestow any part of it on anyone He wishes—but that is His business, not ours. Our job is to be faithful and to put Him first.

Proverbs 11:28 says, "He who trusts in his riches will fall, but the righteous will flourish like the green leaf." When you trust in the Lord and pursue righteousness you will know a joy and contentment that cannot be equaled by *anything* this world has to offer.

It is clear from the Bible that all we have comes from God—not only our days upon the earth, but all that we possess. The question is, what will we do with what God has given us? How will we make the proper decisions regarding our money and possessions?

Will we regard our possessions as something we have earned or deserve—and thus believe we can use them however we please? Will we politely acknowledge that God played a role in the blessings we've received—and "tip" Him in token thanks?

Or will we see ourselves as mere stewards of God's gifts and therefore seek to use all we have to further His eternal kingdom?

Before we go any further in responding to these questions, let's turn to the Bible and learn how others viewed their money and possessions.

OBSERVE

Ezekiel 16 tells us that everything the nation of Israel had came from God. But rather than being content with God as her husband, she played the harlot with other nations and their idols, misusing what God had given her to please her lovers.

Consequently, Israel ended up in captivity in Babylon. However, in His grace and goodness, God returned a remnant of His people to their land. So what did they then do with the blessings God once again bestowed upon them?

The book of Malachi gives us insight into that question. It was written after the remnant returned to Jerusalem and about four hundred years before the birth of Jesus Christ. Let's see what we can learn

MALACHI 1:1-2A,11-14

1 The oracle of the word of the LORD to Israel through Malachi.

2 "I have loved you," says the LORD. But you say, "How have You loved us?"

11 "For from the rising of the sun even to its setting, My name will be great among the nations, and in every place incense is going to be offered to My name, and a grain offering that is pure; for My name will be great among the nations," says the LORD of hosts.

12 "But you are profaning it, in that you say, 'The table of

from the people of Israel about God's expectations regarding how we are to use His gifts to us.

Leader: Read aloud Malachi 1:1-2a,11-14. Have the group do the following:
- *Put a triangle over every reference to **the Lord,** including any pronouns.*
- *Circle every reference to **you** and **the people of Israel.***
- *Draw a box around every occurrence of **offering.***

DISCUSS

- Who is speaking in this passage and to whom?

- Do the people receiving the message seem content? Explain your answer.

- What were they offering to God?

- What was their attitude in bringing their offering to God?

• In light of who God is and the fact that His Law commanded that all sacrifices be perfect, how would you characterize their behavior?

• According to verse 14, what are the consequences, if any, for promising something to God, then fulfilling that commitment in a way that is disrespectful to Him?

• What connection do you find between these Scriptures and how most Christians today respond to God's provision? What about their offerings to God? Do you find many believers who are truly content with what God has given them? Explain your answer.

• Do you think God is pleased with what we are giving to Him? Why or why not?

the LORD is defiled, and as for its fruit, its food is to be despised.'

13 "You also say, 'My, how tiresome it is!' And you disdainfully sniff at it," says the LORD of hosts, "and you bring what was taken by robbery and what is lame or sick; so you bring the offering! Should I receive that from your hand?" says the LORD.

14 "But cursed be the swindler who has a male in his flock and vows it, but sacrifices a blemished animal to the Lord, for I am a great King," says the LORD of hosts, "and My name is feared among the nations."

MALACHI 3:7-12

7 "From the days of your fathers you have turned aside from My statutes and have not kept them. Return to Me, and I will return to you," says the LORD of hosts. "But you say, 'How shall we return?'

8 "Will a man rob God? Yet you are robbing Me! But you say, 'How have we robbed You?' In tithes and offerings.

9 "You are cursed with a curse, for you are robbing Me, the whole nation of you!

10 "Bring the whole tithe into the storehouse, so that there may be food in My house, and test Me now in this," says the LORD of hosts,

OBSERVE

Leader: *Read Malachi 3:7-12. Have the group do the following:*

- *Mark every reference to **God** with a triangle.*
- *Circle every reference to **the people,** including the pronouns **you** and **we.***
- *Draw a box around every reference to **tithes** and **offerings.***

DISCUSS

- What did you learn about the people from these verses? Describe their relationship with God.

- What did you learn from marking references to tithes and offerings?

- What did God promise to do if the people would be faithful in their tithes and offerings?

• What does this reveal about God's view of the gifts—the tithes and offerings—of His people?

INSIGHT

The nation of Israel lived under a theocracy; in other words, God ruled as her king. God created the nation of Israel, gave the people their land, and set up a system of law by which they were to be governed. The Levites, one of the tribes comprising this nation, were given no inheritance in the land; rather their responsibility was to preserve knowledge, instruct the people, and maintain the temple with all its services to God and to His people. To finance this, God set up a system of tithing in which the people gave a portion of their harvest or income, which was then brought into the storehouse. Considering the three annual tithes commanded by God, it is estimated that the people were to give approximately 23 percent of their income to the Lord annually.

"if I will not open for you the windows of heaven and pour out for you a blessing until it overflows.

11 "Then I will rebuke the devourer for you, so that it will not destroy the fruits of the ground; nor will your vine in the field cast its grapes," says the LORD of hosts.

12 "All the nations will call you blessed, for you shall be a delightful land," says the LORD of hosts.

PROVERBS 3:9-10

9 Honor the LORD from your wealth and from the first of all your produce;

10 So your barns will be filled with plenty and your vats will overflow with new wine.

OBSERVE

Let's look now at a passage from Proverbs, a book of wisdom written by King Solomon.

Leader: Read Proverbs 3:9-10. Have the group...
- *circle every occurrence of **your.***
- *draw a box around every reference to any form of **material wealth.***
- *underline the word **first.***

DISCUSS

• What are we instructed to do?

• What did you learn from underlining *first?*

• What is the promised outcome of obeying this instruction?

• What parallel do you see between this verse and what you read in Malachi?

• What does this tell you about God's expectation? What does it reveal about His response to those who give from their income or wealth for His purposes?

OBSERVE

Now let's go to the New Testament to see what we can learn about giving.

Leader: Read Mark 12:41-44. Have the group do the following:
- *Draw a triangle over every reference to **Jesus,** including pronouns.*
- *Draw a box around every reference to **money,** including any synonyms or pronouns.*
- *Circle every reference to **the widow.***

DISCUSS

• What was Jesus doing, according to verse 41?

• What does this tell you about Jesus' interest in our giving?

MARK 12:41-44

41 And He sat down opposite the treasury, and began observing how the people were putting money into the treasury; and many rich people were putting in large sums.

42 A poor widow came and put in two small copper coins, which amount to a cent.

43 Calling His disciples to Him, He said to them, "Truly I say to you, this poor widow put in more than all the contributors to the treasury;

44 for they all put in out of their surplus, but she, out of her poverty, put in all she owned, all she had to live on."

• What did you learn about the widow? How did her gift compare with the gifts of the rich people?

• What did her giving reveal about her relationship to the Lord?

• Do you think the widow was content? Explain your answer.

• Did Jesus try to stop her or return her money?

• Why do you think this incident is mentioned by Jesus to His disciples and recorded in two of the Gospels?

• What lessons, if any, can we draw from this passage?

OBSERVE

The apostle Paul endured much suffering
for the furtherance of the gospel, including
hunger and thirst, persecution and slander,
homelessness and shipwreck. To see what
insight we can gain from his example, let's
look at a portion of his letter to the church
at Philippi.

*Leader: Read Philippians 4:10-14. Have the
group...*
- *underline every reference to **Paul**,
  including pronouns.*
- *circle every reference to **the Philippians**, including pronouns.*

DISCUSS

- What did you learn from marking references to Paul in this passage? How would
  you describe his attitude?

- What was Paul's relationship with the
  Philippians?

- What did the Philippians do for Paul?
  And what was his state when they did it?

10 But I rejoiced in
the Lord greatly, that
now at last you have
revived your concern
for me; indeed, you
were concerned
before, but you lacked
opportunity.

11 Not that I speak
from want, for I have
learned to be content
in whatever circum-
stances I am.

12 I know how to get
along with humble
means, and I also
know how to live in
prosperity; in any and
every circumstance I
have learned the secret
of being filled and
going hungry, both of
having abundance and
suffering need.

13 I can do all things through Him who strengthens me.

14 Nevertheless, you have done well to share with me in my affliction.

• What has Paul learned, according to verses 11 and 12? What does he say about contentment?

• In light of verses 11 and 12, what are the "all things" Paul is able to do through Christ? Is he saying he can do anything he wants to?

• What lessons can we learn from Paul's example for our lives today?

PHILIPPIANS 4:15-19

15 You yourselves also know, Philippians, that at the first preaching of the gospel, after I left Macedonia, no church shared with me in the matter of giving and receiving but you alone;

OBSERVE

Leader: Read Philippians 4:15-19. Have the group…

• *circle every reference to **the Philippians,** including pronouns.*
• *underline every reference to **Paul,** including I and me.*
• *draw a box around every reference to **giving** and **the gift,** including any synonyms.*

DISCUSS

• What did you learn from marking the references to Paul?

• What did you learn about the Philippians and their giving?

• What did you learn about giving from this passage?

• According to verse 17, who benefits in giving? How?

• How do you think verse 19 relates to the preceding verses?

• According to what you learned from this passage, does God care about what we give? Explain your answer.

16 for even in Thessalonica you sent a gift more than once for my needs.

17 Not that I seek the gift itself, but I seek for the profit which increases to your account.

18 But I have received everything in full and have an abundance; I am amply supplied, having received from Epaphroditus what you have sent, a fragrant aroma, an acceptable sacrifice, well-pleasing to God.

19 And my God will supply all your needs according to His riches in glory in Christ Jesus.

2 CORINTHIANS 8:1-5

¹ Now, brethren, we wish to make known to you the grace of God which has been given in the churches of Macedonia,

² that in a great ordeal of affliction their abundance of joy and their deep poverty over-flowed in the wealth of their liberality.

³ For I testify that according to their ability, and beyond their ability, they gave of their own accord,

⁴ begging us with much urging for the favor of participation in the support of the saints,

OBSERVE

Now let's turn to the first portion of two key chapters on giving. (We'll study these further next week.)

Leader: Read 2 Corinthians 8:1-5 aloud. Have the group...

- *circle every reference to **the churches of Macedonia,** including pronouns.*
- *draw a box around every word or phrase that refers to **giving.***

DISCUSS

- What did you learn about the churches of Macedonia? What were their circumstances?

- What did you learn about their giving? How is their giving described?

- What did they give first, according to verse 5?

- How do you think the "gift" they gave first related to their support of the saints? Discuss the reason for your answer. If they hadn't given this gift first, do you think they would have given what they did materially? How might the answer help you discern the truth about your own approach to money, possessions, and the quest for contentment?

5 and this, not as we had expected, but they first gave themselves to the Lord and to us by the will of God.

• Why do you suppose God inspired Paul to write about the churches of Macedonia, immortalizing their story in the Bible?

• Does poverty or hardship excuse us from giving?

• From your experience, how does the support of the work of God around the world in our times compare with the generosity of the churches of Macedonia?

• Would you say the churches of Macedonia had found contentment despite their poverty? Explain your answer.

• What is God saying to your heart this week through the ministry of the Holy Spirit? What passages had the most impact on your view of money and possessions?

WRAP IT UP

When it comes to supporting and furthering the family and work of God, do you beg to give to God's work? Or do others have to plead with, bribe, or coerce you to give?

These lessons about money, possessions, and contentment are not easy to embrace, are they? They hit us right in the pocketbook or the billfold. And our response to these truths reveals the true condition of our hearts; we begin to honestly acknowledge where our treasure really is.

Why don't you take a few minutes to sit quietly and think about what you have learned, asking God to reveal your deepest attitudes about money and giving. Then, if the Lord leads, have a time of prayer and thanksgiving for all that He has so generously blessed you with.

What is your attitude about giving financially to the work of the Lord? Do you view it as a burden, an obligation? Do you see it as a means of gaining material rewards from God? Or do you recognize it as a ministry to the saints? Do you see generosity to others for what it truly is— an expression of the unfathomable grace of God?

As we complete our study this week by continuing in 2 Corinthians 8 and 9, you will notice that Paul repeatedly refers to the ministry of giving as *a gracious work*. Watch the phrase carefully and note the awesome privilege and opportunity you can have to bring God glory through your generous giving. You'll understand in a new way what Jesus meant when He said, "It is more blessed to give than to receive" (Acts 20:35).

OBSERVE

As we continue our study of 2 Corinthians, it's important to know that Paul sent Titus to Corinth in order to take up a collection for the saints. The giving of these believers is what he was referring to through his mention of "this gracious work."

Leader: Read 2 Corinthians 8:7-12. Have the group do the following:
- *Circle every reference to **the Corinthians**, including every pronoun that refers to them.*
- *Draw a box around every word or phrase that refers to **giving**, such as **his gracious work**. Also don't miss any pronouns, such as **it** and **this**, that refer to the work of giving.*
- *Mark every occurrence of the word **love** with a heart.*

2 CORINTHIANS 8:7-12

7 But just as you abound in everything, in faith and utterance and knowledge and in all earnestness and in the love we inspired in you, see that you abound in this gracious work also.

8 I am not speaking this as a command, but as proving through the earnestness of others the sincerity of your love also.

9 For you know the grace of our Lord Jesus Christ, that though He was rich, yet for your sake He became poor, so that you through His poverty might become rich.

DISCUSS

• What "gracious work" did Paul want his readers to perform?

• What did you learn from marking the references to the Corinthians?

• According to verse 8, what would be accomplished through this "gracious work"?

• What example of giving has Jesus provided, according to verse 9? What point is Paul making?

• In verses 11-12 what did Paul urge the Corinthians to do and why?

INSIGHT

According to various surveys, those who attend church weekly give only 3.4 percent of their annual income. Total charitable giving by Americans is between 1.6 percent and 2.16 percent of their income. According to a report from the Barna Research Group, 32 percent of evangelicals in America claim to tithe (to give 10 percent of their income to God's work), but only 12 percent actually do so.[1]

• What did you learn from marking *love*?

• If giving "proves" one's love for God and for His people and His work, what does the information in the Insight box reveal about Christians who live in the wealthiest country in the world?

• What does your own giving demonstrate about your love of God?

10 I give my opinion in this matter, for this is to your advantage, who were the first to begin a year ago not only to do this, but also to desire to do it.

11 But now finish doing it also, so that just as there was the readiness to desire it, so there may be also the completion of it by your ability.

12 For if the readiness is present, it is acceptable according to what a person has, not according to what he does not have.

---

[1] Found at www.barna.org.

• In Matthew 25, Jesus said that when He returns He will separate the sheep from the goats. The sheep will receive eternal life, a reward because they cared for others. In caring for others, He said, they were caring for Him. Have you realized that when you give to others, it's really out of love for Him? How might understanding this change a person's attitude toward giving?

• Sometimes we excuse ourselves from giving, saying we cannot afford to give anything that makes a measurable difference. How does verse 12 address this claim?

• Have you, like the Corinthians, ever found yourself in a situation where God prompted you to give but you put it off? Or what has happened when you've obeyed God's prompting to give? Share your experience with the group and tell what you've learned from it.

OBSERVE

Leader: Read 2 Corinthians 8:13-15. This time have the group do the following:

- *Draw a box around* **this** *in verse 13.*
- *Circle every reference to* **the Corinthians** *as before.*
- *Double underline each occurrence of the word* **equality.**

DISCUSS

- What did you learn about giving from these verses? Note where you marked *this* in verse 13, which refers to giving.

- What did you learn from marking *equality*? How is equality attained?

- What insight does verse 15 offer regarding verses 13 and 14?

2 CORINTHIANS 8:13-15

13 For this is not for the ease of others and for your affliction, but by way of equality—

14 at this present time your abundance being a supply for their need, so that their abundance also may become a supply for your need, that there may be equality;

15 as it is written, "He who gathered much did not have too much, and he who gathered little had no lack."

EXODUS 16:12-21

12 "I have heard the grumblings of the sons of Israel; speak to them, saying, 'At twilight you shall eat meat, and in the morning you shall be filled with bread; and you shall know that I am the LORD your God.'"

13 So it came about at evening that the quails came up and covered the camp, and in the morning there was a layer of dew around the camp.

14 When the layer of dew evaporated, behold, on the surface of the wilderness there was a fine flake-like thing, fine as the frost on the ground.

OBSERVE

In 2 Corinthians 8:15 Paul quoted an Old Testament reference from Exodus 16 to make his point. Let's look at the context of the original.

Leader: Read Exodus 16:12-21 aloud and have the group...

- *draw a box around every reference to* **bread, the layer of dew,** *(also called "manna") that the children of Israel were to gather during their time of wandering in the wilderness. Also mark the pronouns referring to it.*
- *draw a squiggly line* ～～～ *under every reference to* **gathering this bread.**

DISCUSS

- In Exodus 16 we find the children of Israel grumbling against God regarding His provision. They are quite discontented. According to the verses you observed, what was His provision? Discuss only what it was, how it was supplied, and when.

• Now discuss God's commands for gathering the manna.

• Why do you suppose some people kept manna for the next day?

• What did this imply about their relationship with God?

15 When the sons of Israel saw it, they said to one another, "What is it?" For they did not know what it was. And Moses said to them, "It is the bread which the LORD has given you to eat.

16 "This is what the LORD has commanded, 'Gather of it every man as much as he should eat; you shall take an omer apiece according to the number of persons each of you has in his tent.'"

17 The sons of Israel did so, and some gathered much and some little.

18 When they measured it with an omer, he who had gathered much had no excess, and he who had gathered little had no lack; every man gathered as much as he should eat.

19 Moses said to them, "Let no man leave any of it until morning."

20 But they did not listen to Moses, and some left part of it until morning, and it bred worms and became foul; and Moses was angry with them.

21 They gathered it morning by morning, every man as much as he should eat; but when the sun grew hot, it would melt.

• Since the Spirit led Paul to quote from Exodus 16 to make his point on giving, what principles can we learn about giving and receiving from this Old Testament passage?

• How could this be applied to investing money while neglecting to give generously to the work of the Lord?

• Have you ever known anyone who chose to invest in the stock market rather than give away his money, only to lose his money when the market fell?

OBSERVE

Let's return to Paul's letter to the church in Corinth to see what else he tells them about the role of giving in the life of a believer.

Leader: Read 2 Corinthians 9:1-6. Have the group do the following:

- *Underline every reference to **Paul**, indicated by the pronouns **I** and **me**.*
- *Circle every reference to **the Corinthians**. Don't forget to mark the pronouns **you** and **your**.*

Leader: Read 2 Corinthians 9:1-6 once more. This time have the group...

- *draw a box around every reference to **the ministry** (of giving) and **the gift**.*
- *double underline each occurrence of the words **prepared** and **unprepared**.*

DISCUSS

- What did you learn from marking the references to Paul and the Corinthians?

2 CORINTHIANS 9:1-6

¹ For it is superfluous for me to write to you about this ministry to the saints;

² for I know your readiness, of which I boast about you to the Macedonians, namely, that Achaia has been prepared since last year, and your zeal has stirred up most of them.

³ But I have sent the brethren, in order that our boasting about you may not be made empty in this case, so that, as I was saying, you may be prepared;

⁴ otherwise if any Macedonians come with me and find you unprepared, we—not

to speak of you—will be put to shame by this confidence.

5 So I thought it necessary to urge the brethren that they would go on ahead to you and arrange beforehand your previously promised bountiful gift, so that the same would be ready as a bountiful gift and not affected by covetousness.

6 Now this I say, he who sows sparingly will also reap sparingly, and he who sows bountifully will also reap bountifully.

• What did you learn from marking the references to giving, the ministry to the saints?

• Have you been encouraged by hearing about others' experiences in giving? How?

• What did you learn from marking *prepared* and *unprepared*? What did Paul want the believers in Corinth to be prepared to do?

• What was Paul's concern for the Corinthians? What danger did he mention in verse 5? How would this affect their giving?

• What principle of giving did you learn from verse 6?

• What did you learn from this passage that is applicable to your life?

OBSERVE

Leader: *Read 2 Corinthians 9:7-15. Have the group...*

- *circle every reference to **the Corinthians,** including **each one** and **you.***
- *draw a box around every reference to **giving,** including words like **ministry** and **liberality.***
- *mark every reference to **God the Father** and **Jesus, the Son of God** with a triangle:* △

DISCUSS

- From the references you marked, what did you observe about God and about the Corinthians in respect to giving?

- Look back at the references to the ministry of giving. What did you learn from marking these? How are the Corinthians equipped for giving?

- According to 2 Corinthians 9:7-15, what does bountiful, or generous, giving bring? Make sure you cover the text carefully, as you don't want to miss a thing.

2 CORINTHIANS 9:7-15

7 Each one must do just as he has purposed in his heart, not grudgingly or under compulsion, for God loves a cheerful giver.

8 And God is able to make all grace abound to you, so that always having all sufficiency in everything, you may have an abundance for every good deed;

9 as it is written, "He scattered abroad, he gave to the poor, His righteousness endures forever."

10 Now He who supplies seed to the sower and bread for food will supply and multiply your seed for sowing and increase the harvest of your righteousness;

11 you will be enriched in everything for all liberality, which through us is producing thanksgiving to God.

12 For the ministry of this service is not only fully supplying the needs of the saints, but is also overflowing through many thanksgivings to God.

13 Because of the proof given by this ministry, they will glorify God for your obedience to your confession of the gospel of Christ and for the liberality of your contribution to them and to all,

14 while they also, by prayer on your behalf, yearn for you because of the surpassing grace of God in you.

• What did you learn from these verses about the importance of the heart of the giver?

• Do you think most people today see giving as a ministry, a joy? Do we tend to recognize giving as something that brings glory to God because of the thanksgiving it produces? Explain your answers.

• According to verse 13, what is the connection between giving and one's confession, or belief, in the gospel of Christ?

• The word *grace*—which indicates God's unmerited favor, His bountiful gift of the New Covenant with all its benefits—is mentioned in verses 8 and 14. What does giving demonstrate about grace?

• How did Paul tie grace with giving in verse 15? What is God's indescribable gift?

15 Thanks be to God for His indescribable gift!

OBSERVE

As we wrap up our study of giving, let's look at one more example of heartfelt generosity. The passage you're about to read took place shortly before Jesus was crucified for the sins of the world.

Leader: Read Mark 14:3-9. Have the group...
  • *circle every reference to **the woman**, including pronouns.*
  • *draw a box around every reference to **the perfume.***

3 While He was in Bethany at the home of Simon the leper, and reclining at the table, there came a woman with an alabaster vial of very costly perfume of pure nard; and she broke the vial and poured it over His head.

4 But some were indignantly remarking to one another, "Why has this perfume been wasted?

5 "For this perfume might have been sold for over three hundred denarii, and the money given to the

INSIGHT

A denarius was equivalent to a day's wages. Therefore, the woman's gift, invested in perfume, was equal to almost a year's wages.

poor." And they were scolding her.

6 But Jesus said, "Let her alone; why do you bother her? She has done a good deed to Me.

7 "For you always have the poor with you, and whenever you wish you can do good to them; but you do not always have Me.

8 "She has done what she could; she has anointed My body beforehand for the burial.

9 "Truly I say to you, wherever the gospel is preached in the whole world, what this woman has done will also be spoken of in memory of her."

DISCUSS

• What did you learn from marking the references to the perfume? How was it described?

• How did Jesus respond to the woman's gift? Why?

• What is a lasting effect of this woman's generosity?

• What does this tell you about Jesus' attitude, His attention to our giving?

• According to verse 8, to what extent had the woman given?

• This woman gave her all while she could. She didn't miss her opportunity, and she held nothing back. Can your efforts in giving be described in the same way?

• What was the most significant insight you gained this week in respect to your own life and the awesome ministry of giving? As this week comes to a close, share how God has spoken to your heart.

WRAP IT UP

It is our prayer that, of all the truths you've learned through this study, you grasp the awesome honor, the incredible privilege, of being a co-laborer with God in kingdom work. Many organizations in the world are devoted to meeting the physical needs of mankind, but who will care for their souls? If we address people's bodily needs but neglect their souls, what will it profit them? They must encounter Jesus—God's only begotten Son—without whom they will perish.

Our giving should enable us not only to reach the lost but also to minister to the needs of the saints, support the work of ministry, and make disciples of all nations. All true ministry is founded on the need for believers to know and obey the whole counsel of God so that they might walk in an intimate, vital, confident relationship with their Creator.

How important it is to "put our money where our mouth is." If we say we love Jesus and the people of God, let us prove it through our giving. May we do what we can with what we have while there is time.

May God cleanse our hearts of the covetousness that leads us to waste money on the temporal while neglecting the eternal. And may we realize that with the receiving of every gift thanksgiving fills the heavens, ascending past Satan's principalities and powers right to the very throne of God—the One alone to whom belongs all praise, honor, glory, power, and dominion. When the Spirit of God has dominion over all our monies, all our possessions, then and only then will we know contentment.

Oh beloved of God, in what ways are you saying, "Thanks be to God for His indescribable gift"?

Give, and it will be given to you.

They will pour into your lap a good measure—pressed down, shaken together, and running over.

For by your standard of measure it will be measured to you in return.

LUKE 6:38

FOR FURTHER READING

The Law of Rewards: Giving What You Can't Keep to Gain What You Can't Lose by Randy Alcorn. Generous Giving Series. Wheaton, IL: Tyndale House Publishers, 2003.

The Eternity Portfolio: A Practical Guide to Investing Your Money for Ultimate Results by Alan Gotthardt. Generous Giving Series. Wheaton, IL: Tyndale House Publishers, 2003.

Whose Money Is It Anyway? A Biblical Guide to Using God's Wealth by John MacArthur. Nashville: Word Publishing, 2000.

This unique Bible study series from Kay Arthur and the teaching team of Precept Ministries International tackles the issues with which inquiring minds wrestle—in short, easy-to-grasp lessons ideal for small-group settings. The study courses in the series can be followed in any order. Here is one possible sequence:

How Do You Know God's Your Father?

by Kay Arthur, David and BJ Lawson

So many say "I'm a Christian," but how can they really know God's their Father—and that heaven's home? The short book of 1 John was written for that purpose—that you might *know* that you really do have eternal life. This is a powerful, enlightening study that will take you out of the dark and open your understanding to this key biblical truth.

Having a Real Relationship with God

by Kay Arthur

For those who yearn to know God and relate to Him in meaningful ways, Kay Arthur opens the Bible to show the way to salvation. With a straightforward examination of vital Bible passages, this enlightening study focuses on where we stand with God, how our sin keeps us from knowing Him, and how Christ bridged the chasm between humans and their Lord.

Being a Disciple: Counting the Real Cost

by Kay Arthur, Tom and Jane Hart

Jesus calls His followers to be disciples. And discipleship comes with a cost, a commitment. This study takes an inductive look at how the

Bible describes a disciple, sets forth the marks of a follower of Christ, and invites students to accept the challenge and then enjoy the blessings of discipleship.

How Do You Walk the Walk You Talk?
by Kay Arthur

This thorough, inductive study of Ephesians 4 and 5 is designed to help students see for themselves what God says about the lifestyle of a true believer in Jesus Christ. The study will equip them to live in a manner worthy of their calling, with the ultimate goal of developing a daily walk with God marked by maturity, Christlikeness, and peace.

Living a Life of True Worship
by Kay Arthur, Bob and Diane Vereen

Worship is one of Christianity's most misunderstood topics. This study explores what the Bible says about worship—what it is, when it happens, where it takes place. Is it based on your emotions? Is it something that only happens on Sunday in church? Does it impact how you serve? This study offers fresh, biblical answers.

Discovering What the Future Holds
by Kay Arthur, Georg Huber

With all that's transpiring in the world, people cannot help but wonder what the future holds. Will there ever be peace on earth? How long will the world live under the threat of terrorism? Is a one-world ruler on the horizon? This easy-to-use study guide leads readers through the book of Daniel, which sets forth God's blueprints for the future.

How to Make Choices You Won't Regret
by Kay Arthur, David and BJ Lawson
Every day we face innumerable decisions, some of which have the
potential to change the course of our lives forever. Where do we go for
direction? What do we do when faced with temptation? This fast-
moving study offers practical, trustworthy guidelines by exploring the
role of Scripture and the Holy Spirit in the decision-making process.

Building a Marriage That Really Works
by Kay Arthur, David and BJ Lawson
God designed marriage to be a satisfying, fulfilling relationship, and
He created men and women so that they—together, and as one flesh—
could reflect His love for the world. Marriage, when lived out as God
intended, makes us complete, it brings us joy, and gives our lives fresh
meaning. In this study, readers examine God's design for marriage and
learn how to establish and maintain the kind of marriage that brings
lasting joy.

How Can a Man Control His Thoughts, Desires, and Passions?
by Bob Vereen
This study equips men with the truth that God has provided everything we need to resist temptation. Through the examples of men in
Scripture—those who fell into sin and those who stood firm—readers
will find hope for controlling their passions, learn how to choose the
path of purity, and find assurance that through the power of the Holy
Spirit and God's Word, they can stand before God blameless and pure.

Living Victoriously in Difficult Times

by Kay Arthur, Bob and Diane Vereen

We live in a fallen world filled with fallen people, and we cannot escape hardship and pain. Somehow difficult times are a part of God's plan and they serve His purposes. This study helps readers discover how to glorify God in the midst of their pain. They'll learn how to find joy even when life seems unfair and experience the peace that comes from trusting in the One whose strength is made perfect in their weaknesses.

ABOUT THE AUTHORS

KAY ARTHUR, executive vice president and cofounder of Precept Ministries International, is known around the world as a Bible teacher, author, conference speaker, and host of the national radio and television programs *Precepts for Life*.

Kay and her husband, Jack, founded Precept Ministries in 1970 in Chattanooga, Tennessee. Started as a fledgling ministry for teens, Precept today is a worldwide outreach that establishes children, teens, and adults in God's Word, so that they can discover the Bible's truths for themselves. Precept inductive Bible studies are taught in all 50 states. The studies have been translated into 67 languages, reaching 120 countries.

DAVID ARTHUR is a teaching elder and assistant pastor at Lookout Mountain Presbyterian Church outside Chattanooga, Tennessee. He holds a master's degree from Reformed Theological Seminary.